American Happiness

Jacqueline Allen Trimble

AMERICAN
HAPPINESS

NewSouth Books
Montgomery

NewSouth Books
105 S. Court Street
Montgomery, AL 36104

Publisher's Cataloging-in-Publication Data

Trimble, Jacqueline Allen
American happiness / Jacqueline Allen Trimble
p. cm

ISBN 978-1-58838-327-3 (hardcover)
ISBN 978-1-60306-420-0 (ebook)

1. Poetry. I. Title.

2016949493

Design by Randall Williams and Kate Longaker

Printed in the United States of America

ACKNOWLEDGMENTS
"American Happiness" was published in *Blue Lake Review*. A version of "The
Klan Panhandles for Donations at the Intersection of Court Street and the Southern
Bypass," as "Alms," was published in *The Griot*, Fall 1999. A version of "Second
Sight" was published in *The Griot*, Fall 1999. "How to Survive as a Black Woman
Everywhere in America Including the Deep South," appears on the website Perils
and Perks of Privilege—White, Project Humanities, Arizona State University.
"Ethnophaulism for the News" appeared in *The Offing*, a channel of the Los
Angeles Review of Books, September 17, 2015, online. "Lineage" appeared in
The New Sound.

For my husband, Joseph, with love.

Thank you for saving my life.

CONTENTS

How My Mother Taught Me to Write Poems

MY MOTHER WAS A foot soldier in the fight for civil rights, had a cross burned on her lawn, drove students to Lanier, a local high school, to integrate it, and was sued along with CBS for comments she made on television. She was unafraid, dignified, and determined. My mother was never loud. I don't remember her ever raising her voice, but she had a way of saying things that made the listener acquiesce. All the black women of that generation I knew could do that. They might have used the interrogative form, but there was never any doubt of the command underneath the question. When my mother asked, "Are you wearing that?" or "Are you speaking to me?" I immediately changed into something more presentable or altered my tone.

She could spell most any word, having studied Latin for seven years and translated Julius Caesar's battles. "Don't say *Massatwosette*s like the governor," she would say, "Say, *Massachusetts*," emphasizing the *chew* in the middle. "Do not imitate these little white children you go to school with and those awful twangs. You must speak well." She liked curse words, but only in private and among very close friends. And whoever received the largesse of her choice words knew that he or she been cussed. She reminded me that though she was a widow woman raising a child on her own, we could never be poor because we were educated and had come from a long line of educated and refined people who had never bowed to anyone and never would. When a professor used me as an example, suggesting my grandfather surely had been a sharecropper, she said, "You tell him your grandfather was a teacher and a storeowner. He and your grandmother recited poetry to their children. They owned their own land, had a painted house, and the first car of anyone, black or white, in the community."

In the fall of 1968, I went to Edward T. Davis Elementary. My mother made sure of it. My father had died earlier that year, and my mother, who was actually my stepmother, was determined to raise me as she thought my father would have wanted. That meant I was going to get the best education she could find. I was going to be well-rounded. I would take ballet and piano and belong to social clubs to learn decorum. And though I was more of a tomboy than a princess, I was going to be a lady. Most of all, I was going to know that I was as smart, as worthy, and as good as any other human in this world or the next, despite any messages I would get from some in Montgomery, Alabama.

So, I became the only black child in Davis Elementary that year. I joined the Brownies, and my mother joined the PTA. Whatever minor skirmishes or major wars ensued behind my being at that school, I never heard of them. In those days, children minded children's business and adults minded their own. Neither inquired about the doings of the other. What I do know is that fall my mother volunteered to read palms at the fall festival. Dressed in a long flowing skirt and a peasant blouse, she played the part of fortune teller. Children and adults alike entered her small booth to have Mama gaze into her magic eight ball and tell their future. I went dressed as a ghost. There I was. The only little black child in the whole school wandering the halls of the festival in a sheet with a pointed pillow case hat in which my mother had cut two little eyeholes. It was years before I understood why my mother laughed and laughed and took so many pictures of me in my white sheet that night. Even then she was teaching me the power and pleasure of ironic juxtaposition—a lesson that continues to inform my sense of humor as well as my poetry.

CLOSURE

EVERYBODY IN AMERICA HATE THE SOUTH

That land filled to the rafters
with ghosts of lynched boys and attics full
of souvenirs—dried ears, fingers, genitalia
like prunes—the sweet Magnolia memory
of Miss Scarlett calling for Mammy who
has now grown some dreadlocks and owns
the chicken restaurant on the boulevard.
America ought to say
thank you, Miss South, thank you for being like
Jesus and taking on the sins of the whole country
or being our crazy Aunt Hazel who runs naked
through a house full of company shouting
all the foolish things we think but can't say
so we can walk around all post-racial
and watch *Gone With the Wind* over and over
swooning from the romance.

CLOSURE

The summer my father planted grapevines,
we lived with our mouths in expectant hollows,
imagined rich fruit cool against our tongues.
We moved among the rows and whispered praises
to flat young leaves spreading out like fans.
And when the land sank in and drew the vines,
the tendrils like wilted curls, we kicked the dirt—
our flimsy hope shifting like air—and pulled
the disappointment around us as shawls.

But my father took his liquor to the vineyard
and drank a toast to his undoing. He took his sacrament
in faith until his soul was renewed. That night,
he plowed up the whole north field, straight through
the place we buried things, the weak pups, the runts.
The bones turned up with earth, rising from the dead,
as if they wished to touch again
the thin life unraveled with each breath.
My father cried, as always when he drank,
and knelt among the scattered bones. The leaves
of the pear tree descended like spirits. The fruit,
not yet ripe, bobbed like unlit lanterns.

He watched his breath unravel,
fly from him like dander. He might have caught it
had he not been clutching at his heart. The strong fingers

indented the muscle until he kissed the ground
in one last prayer. He could not take back
the work, the used up beats of his life.
He could not even keep the blood
that ran across his lip. Much later,
I read about a girl who saw her father
kill himself and then could not forgive
the amaryllis on the table, the giving up,
and oh, like that, the life wasted from him.
And if I could plow through earth
and touch my father, call back his spirit
and his flesh, I would tell him this,
then press my thumbs against his air
and kill him at my leisure.

SECOND SIGHT

I

Let the spirits gather here
in my mother's eye. Let some
moonstruck apparition walk her
into the eternal. Three days
the dogs will bark at our door.
And the old women sing,
their voices smooth as ruby
elixir, their tobacco skins soft
as clay. Let her sickness depart.
Let morphine days vaporize
like breath in winter. Let the preacher
say the end. Tell him pour the wine,
the blood. Let her earthly dreams
be finished. Come, gather
beneath the swollen moon and touch
this life, fragile and resilient as skin.

II

My mother swears
that death walked in her room
last night, smiled at her and shook
her foot. But I bear witness
only to the scream that shook the house
and each day's obituary
of sudden causes.

III

The lamp shines
on her distended face. I listen
for each breath that rattles,
spirit in a sack. Esprit, aspire, expire.
Expiration date unknown. She has come
to this. The old ways will not come to me.
My palms turn outward and prayers fall through
my open hands. Old women sing.
I hiss at the moon and pray for sight:
      Wondrous and mystic light,
      embrace my soul,
      inflame my vacant eye.

THE DAY AFTER HER MOTHER DIED

She cannot wash the dish.
Even the bowl is too full of an egg yellow
she and her mother wore to a recital
in the park. If she looks closely
she can see lace forming
in the suds. Some thing, small and hard,
rises in her chest. She imagines
she can take a knife and with one stroke
divide herself.

"No such luck," her mother would have said.

Instead, she settles for immobility,
and there she stands, her gown soaked
with dishwater, the bowl still
in her hand. Visitors come.

"Like clockwork," her mother would have said.

Their hands are always full—
money, casseroles, prayers.
"We are sorry for your loss," they say,
as if they cannot guess she is sorry too.
Between the visits, she waits
and waits for whatever comes next.

"A watched pot never boils," her mother would have said.

Will someone, you perhaps,
step out of the shadows of this house,
seize this girl, and fold her in your arms,
especially some night when she lies sweating
afraid of the silence in the next room?

THE RELATIVITY OF MIDLIFE

When I was young, time was a desert stretching to the sea. A taste
for salt and cowrie shells kept me on the move. Some days there
were windstorms. Some days no oasis in sight. But everything
was poetry, even the parched lips of camels, the sway of their
haunches rhythmic as sex. Once, a plane fell from the sky, its
wide hawk-like shadow foretelling the end of the story. Another
traveler's head caught the burning fuselage. To me, the blast was
a firecracker, the buzz of a distant fly. I lay in tents woven of goat
hair, wishing on the flecks in my lover's eyes. Smells of roasted
meat lingered in the air, on my fingers. My belly full to bursting
with wine and dates too. Soon I would learn, most nights hold
nothing but hard earth, and still I desired this journey to last and
last.

Someday came. The sea appeared beyond a random dune, and I
discovered time is yesterday when I lifted my water-skin for a sip,
my two year old daughter tugging the knee of my jeans. When I
put the bottle down, she was twenty-four. By the time we loped
to the parking lot, she was fifty. Dutifully, I lay down in the car I
had driven to the seashore. It now led a winding caravan. A short
journey really, the future and present already gone, points folded
onto what seemed a far horizon, a single step away all the while.

DID JEAN PAUL SARTRE EVER ASK SIMONE DE BEAUVOIR TO GO TO THE WINN-DIXIE?

You can bleed in a war and earn a medal.
  I can bleed in a war and earn a medal
  and I can bleed for three, five, eight days
  every month
  for forty years
  and live.

You can pee standing up.
  I can pee standing up
  and frequently do squatting over a suspect toilet
  after waiting in the women's room line
  the pee skeeting out of me like water from a blocked hose
  running down my thigh as I grab for tissue that is not there
  or scoop urine frantically back up my leg
  a wayward stream already puddling in my shoe
  clean myself and the floor in three minutes or less
  with a napkin from Burger King dug out of my purse
  and walk out of the stall composed and unstained like
  a lady.

You can throw a basketball through a hoop.
  I can throw a basketball through a hoop
  and ensure the survival of the species by incubating
  a basketball-sized human being in my uterus
  for almost ten months my tits filling exponentially with milk,

water balloons ready for the sweet hurl of release,
my bladder squished by the weight of procreation,
hemorrhoids hanging out my ever-expanding ass
yet craving Taco Bell barely beef burritos
which I will eat and puke up in the parking lot
before going home and being repulsed
by the smell of the Irish Spring soap
you insist on bathing with (even though
I have asked you repeatedly to stop creating smells)
and puke again while I cook chicken casserole
between trips to the john
until the moment the hand of God squeezes my gut
and I go down on my knees, on my back, squatting in a field,
water, jello and pass one of you
through a ten-centimeter canal of softened hip bones,
out my grateful vagina
and live.

You can run a corporation or a country
    I can run a corporation or a country
    and lead a Brownie troop on an expedition through the woods
    where I will get Lyme disease
    and have to take strong antibiotics
    which make me nauseous and miserable
    but not enough to stop me
    from chairing the PTA clothing swap,
    raising $10,000 for a gym floor
    before doing the grocery shopping at the Winn-Dixie
    where my obsessive coupon clipping saves us $7,000

so I can afford to get my hair done and a mani-pedi
(after I have cooked the children's dinner and found them
an appropriate babysitter) to look beautiful enough to impress
your co-workers at the party I will attend, smiling gracefully
between trips to the bathroom to pump milk for the baby,
puke from the antibiotics and pee as well as I can,
navigating a tight dress and tortuous undergarments,
then emerge from the stall like
a lady.

A FEAST WITH THE SANE

My brother has gone mad.
He smokes and smokes and smokes.
He laughs and dances, dances and laughs.
Sometimes he whispers to himself.
Nobody takes a crazy man without proof.
We need him to confess
to say, "I have lost all reason.
Do with me what you will."

We sit around my mother's kitchen table.
"Will you confess?" we ask. "Will you confess
your illness?" His cigarettes ash slowly. The smoke
makes languid curls about our heads. "Confess," we shout
"or your mother will cry." Light from the TV
brightens our faces. Three men have beaten
a grandmother to death. A woman sold her child
for crack. A blonde girl has not been seen for weeks.
The neighbors search for what remains. Perhaps,
she will appear in a bar, on a subway, her own bed.
Who would do such a thing? She was so good.
Between the little dramas, my mother offers
heaping plates of food. "Eat something," she says.
She buys white sneakers in blue boxes
from the Home Shopping Network,
piles them in my brother's room.
His room is like a shoe store. She buys

cigarettes in long green cartons,
piles them in his room. His room is like a cigarette store.
"Don't smoke in the house," she chimes.

"Will you confess?" we say again.
My brother laughs and dances, dances and laughs.
Once he danced and laughed so much,
three deacons, unaccustomed to such joyful noise,
led him from the sanctuary into the bright sunshine
of the parking lot. Their hands were kind.
Their anointed eyes were resolute.
"We will pray for you," they said, then left him there
among his voices, the only choir he would need,
and the shining cars.

"Will you confess?" we ask again.
My brother laughs and dances, dances and laughs.
Outside in the cul-de-sac, around and around he goes.
"Eat something," my mother yells again,
as if he is an honored guest
at the neighbor's barbeque. Instead, he pees.
Pees and laughs. "Don't stain your sneakers!"
my mother calls. The neighbors watch as patient as assassins.
Their eyes fill with pee.
"Will you confess?" they ask.
They laugh and dance, dance and laugh
in their shining family rooms. Through the windows
shine five hundred dramas in high definition.
What madness first imagined suffering

packaged, sold, and piped through a wall?
Around and around we go.

I dream.
We are at a barbeque.
The smoke makes languid curls above our heads.
We are dancing, dancing and laughing.
We dance across the neighbors' yards.
Beside a yellow lake, we laugh and dance.
The neighbors smile at us.
They pile great heaps of food on paper plates.
My brother, unaccustomed to so many kindly eyes,
leads himself out of this sanctuary
into the bright sunshine of the cul-de-sac.
He does not stop. He runs and runs.
His white sneakers flash in the settling darkness.

He leaps some bodies lying in the street.
"As patient as assassins," he says.
Their voices rise and curl inside his head.
I catch him in a distant alleyway.
The yellow walls go up and up and up.
I want to say, "You will be all right." I want to say,
"You will get better."
Instead, I dish up his plate, a single human eye,
"Come," I say, "Feast with the sane."

THINGS THAT ARE LOST

Like a sock in the dryer
like mercy on a sloth
like the yellow buzz of summer
when winter comes
like your steady breath on my neck
when we awaken
I have lost the sound
of my mother's voice.

If objects in motion remain in motion
until some force stops them
what force stops our memory of the dead?

IF I DIDN'T WRITE POETRY

Maybe robbing banks is my true calling.
And instead of making poems, I should
learn to dodge surveillance cameras, put on
a disguise. Tortoise shell shades.

I could take a dog with me, and a cane.
Nobody would suspect a blind woman.
I might hire an accomplice named
Fred, to drive the getaway car. An inconspicuous
Prius. Even crooks can love the environment.

I tap my way across the lobby
with my fake seeing-eye dog
Lester. I smile at the teller, reach into my raincoat—
Oh, yeah. It would have to be raining
for atmosphere—then give her my note.
Perhaps something in iambic pentameter.
Better yet, heroic couplets:
Please give me all the money in your till,
So no one in this bank I'll have to kill.
(You can see why the bank robbing
might work out better than the poetry.)

Wait, I forgot the gun. I hate guns,
but a bank robber must do what a poet only imagines.
I point a plastic (yet convincing) .38 at her,

hand her the couplets, take the money,
and Lester and I hightail it out to Fred, waiting

in a pink Cadillac.

So damn foolish. Well,
doing two to ten will give me time
to rework my sonnets and villanelles.

CHURCH WOMEN

The roll of the eyes, and the click
of the razor tongue, that smile
all sweetness of switchblade.
One hand take your gum.
One hand hold fast to Jesus.
Nobody do nice nasty
like church women do.

The preacher preach and preach and preach.
Well-a-hun-a hun-a hun
yeeeeessssss
A hun-a hun-a hun
Jeessusss.
The children sleep good.
Fried chicken rise like Satan
from the fellowship hall.

They eye you over spoonfuls.
Size up your righteousness
with each dip. Double ham hocks
for Brother this. One little drummette
for Sister that.
Your mouth water so
feels like sacrilege or dancing in the spirit.

Peach cobbler, *praise the Lord,*
rutabaga, yams, candied
and casseroled, collard greens,
mustard greens, turnip greens,
Oooh, Lawd
black eyed peas, butter
beans, yeast rolls,

neck bones,
pig ears, Watergate salad, ham
and *No*
you may not
have more mac and cheese
until all are served
praise God!

FAT RELIGION

Woody Allen philosophized
God may be in fat,
in some thick cell clinging
to a thigh or belly.
His point was this:
what we lose in width
we may lose in soul as well.

Sundays, I work the treadmill
every joint in my body longs for youth
or the stop button. Each step feels
a march toward hell or heresy.
And who is god of fat?
Some lesser demigod with high hopes?
What obese Titan rocks above us all
his tiny heart aflutter under avoirdupois?
Has he sent us John the Baptist
with a knack for sales,
hawking a svelte salvation
proselytizing promises of tight abs,
firm butts, arms like steel levers?

No thanks. I want no false prophet
guarantee to melt away my soul in thirty days.

Oh, let me be a martyr
among these thin and famished sinners.
Let me eat my cake
and have it too.
Let my soul grow so large
fitting through the door
is well beyond my power
Then I will pray like Saint Joan burning,
surrounded by my own
state of grace.

FAMILY PHOTOGRAPH: A CONJUGATION

I am standing in a doorway. My dress is blue.
My hair swept up like hope. You stand beside me,
young and thin. You hold our new son, a bright penny.
She is there too, her head thrown back in laughter, her hands
in her pockets. It is Christmas.
We do not know this will be her last. You never know.
You cannot know.
They tell you everything but this.

THE GEOGRAPHY
OF PASSION

CINDERELLA FINDS HAPPINESS
WITH HER THIRD HUSBAND

There are no fairies in fairy tales.
That should have been a clue,
but her nature was romantic
her stepmother wicked,
two half-sisters, both cruel and ugly.
Same old, same old. So,
after one moonlit stroll and a missing slipper,
she married in haste and then repented.
What a prince! Who would have thought caps could hide
the incisors of a wolf? Soon, he vanished
like fairy dust on the stroke of midnight.

Next time, not for love, but money.
She didn't even mind his troll-like looks.
His heart was kind, so she made a life
of tender words and pretty things
until he lay down and never rose again.
Heart failure, they supposed.
Following the usual instructions,
she lit every candle in the kingdom,
pronounced a brief incantatory spell
and kissed his dead lips gently
but he stayed dead.
Too much kindness and not enough
true love to pump the blood.

Cinderella Finds Happiness with Her Third Husband

She buried him in his blue serge.
The perfect shade of steel coffin.

Fairytales tell a true story,
if only she had known how to read.

Once upon a time, love came
and brought a dowry of dragon fire,
poison apples, one hundred years of sleep
for the whole town. On a good day,
a glass coffin courtesy of the wicked.
Quest-worthy and quick,
love made a golden chalice.
To find it, she will trade her voice for silence,
her strong tail for thin hairy legs
which must be shaved regularly and well.
Each step will be a torture of pins
or glass shards. At the climax
she will tiptoe through the world
to see her heart's desire waltz
a woman full of words and with hairy gams
into the sunset. Background music
sure to get copious play time and awards
swells as she sinks teary-eyed into the sea
Not a dry eye in sight.

See girl, it never turns out well.
Some woman drowned at the bottom of the sea
frozen in an alleyway, her heels or arms or head

hacked off, tortured to death
by a stepdaughter's momentary beauty.
Why look for happy endings there? Try this:

Third time, charming.
One day in the supermarket
long after she had bartered rose-colored glasses
for bifocals and good wine,
magic happened around the eggplant bin.
She found his little paunch endearing. He liked
her red stilettos. *Old dogs can and do*, she thought.
Can and do.

THE GEOGRAPHY OF PASSION

A woman steps off the Paris metro straight into
the love of her life. The audience sighs with envy.
Would this scene work in Des Moines?
Is there a man on the *Champs-Élysées* longing
for cornfields, weary of passing time
in the same patisserie?
Does his wife dream of men
who sound like
Mississippi, those long, flat vowels
drawling her to ecstasy?

Say Bergman had walked down a landing strip in
Cleveland, would we still remember this,
the shifting fog of an Ohio evening filling us with ennui?
Or if Harry had met Sally at a swap meet
in Greenville, would her orgasmic interlude delight
the lunch crowd at Miss Ludie's Family Buffet?

My husband turns to me in bed one night,
his lips so wanton the camera would cut away
to crashing waves or a tunnel-piercing train.
Is it wrong to prefer sleep?
Would I turn to him an eager ingénue,
our passion the bright flame of a thousand
lights, if outside my window lay the Seine,
and not the Alabama?

INCANTATION

Let the dishes go unwashed,
and the children uncalled. Let them run forever

through pools of streetlight. Put the dog out
and let the cat go too. Unhinge our house
and come to me:

mountain, blue, cup, lush,
blossom, fire, kumquat, tongue,
mango, mouth, sassafras, maroon.

Open me
a ripe papaya.

SO MUCH THAT FASCINATES IS THE BLOOD

On the Roman ruins I stand
where Julius Caesar stood
and where he went down,
astonished at his own blood,
and wonder if he had imagined me
as I now imagine him.
What would his ghost say to me
or to the Italian boys who
breached the high gate
and tagged the ancient wall
in a vulgar tongue?

On a Mobile, Alabama, street
a boy once walked. His summer evening
ambushed by boots and fists.
The marker tells the tale.
And I wonder if he, astonished
at his fate, thought of Caesar
their sacrificial blood yoked
by the treachery of countrymen,
their stories told and retold
to passersby and tourists
in a common tongue?

LINEAGE

My father was a thin brown line
an arrow shot through her body
on its way somewhere else. And nothing
could stop his trajectory. And nothing
could bring him back. Not her love, as sharp
as paper's edge, not her swelling belly,
not the word my grandmother named her
when she threw her out. If only he had loved her enough
to set her on fire and leave her ash on the empty altar,
instead of alone.
This is the story my mother tells me
the first time we meet. She tells it again the next time.
And will again for years. How her sister came to get her,
how hate sustained her, how she wrapped me
in a blanket and gave me away.
What can I do for her? What can I do?

THE RETORT I WISH I HAD MADE AFTER I FORGOT TO PACK YOUR FAVORITE TRUNKS ON A FAMILY TRIP TO THE GULF OF MEXICO AND YOU CALLED ME TRIFLING

The *argiope aurantia* waits
all day to catch a creature
so enamored of the garden, he sees too late
that some silken caresses are full
of venom. She enrobes his dying body
in her web, then eats him when she pleases.
His carcass serves up warning
to trod the careful path.

The *platymeris biguttata* bites
enough to leave a scar,
and once, almost killed
an entomologist. The man meant no harm,
but reaching in to clean its habitat,
overstepped a boundary. It bit
the feeding hand. A trifle, really,
but larger than the tiny flea
that brought the whole of Europe
to its knees.

Some parasitoids, tiny wasps or flies
head of a pin, thumbnail trifles
are big enough to be ungrateful guests. They enter

the very bodies of their hosts and leave
unwelcome gifts
eggs, not Fabergé,
eggs that hatch and eat the hosts
from within. Some things insignificant
should not be trifled with.

Need I recount Goliath's thudding fall?

So, when you name me, *Trifling,*
How shall I respond?
With caresses,
with gratitude,
or gifts?

WE ARE IN COZUMEL

We are in Cozumel.
The guide says call him
"Geraldo." He is tan and large. His accent
sounds fake. Maybe he is a college student
named Fred from Philadelphia.
"If your mask fills with water," he says,
"lift, blow it out, and put it back on."
"Do they sanitize these things?"
I ask as I pick mine from the trough.
"Seawater kills bacteria," my friend says.
Like she knows. I pray and put it on.
The flippers too. Fungus cream looms
like a cautionary tale. My friend
dolphins her way behind Geraldo-Fred.
I float near the children. Tethered
by their mothers' gaze, they dart
as if they've never left the sea. A good time
until I begin to drown.
The couple with the life buoy
is ten feet away. The gulf swallows my cry
for help and takes me far from shore. The sun glints
on my friend's happy blonde head.
Nothing but a sunken Jesus in her sights. He reaches up
to her through waves and fish.
                            At the service
the choir will sing "Precious Lord."

My students will come. My coworkers too.
Even the ones who don't like me. There will be
a huge picture of me surrounded by white roses
and hydrangea, the sharks having swallowed
me whole.
                    But, I do not drown.
The couple hears me. The guide returns
and swims me back to the shore where
portly businessmen, old ladies who nap and read,
and bikini-clad teens await
the skin cancer in their future.

HOW A WOMAN CARVES POETRY OF HER BONES

She is standing on an auction block
or lying in a strange bed
or walking down a river path
or eating guava with salt
or suckling a sick child
or fashioning a thatched roof
or reading of a killed boy
or opening a love letter
or drinking gin in Louisville
or praying at her mother's wake
or harvesting an okra pod
or loving on a good man
or tending to a small fire
or washing off a brown boot
or dozing on a screened porch
or cutting biscuits with a cup
or dreaming of another life
when she stops and takes the knife.

A WOMAN EXPLAINS THE WORLD
TO HER CHILDREN

The world does not owe you
indigo, the quiet charm
of purple love. Lie down and see.
Manna will not fall
to fill your anxious belly.
No matter how many stars
you wish on, those distant suns
flamed out long ago.
Your comfort is built
on someone's broken back.
Even if it's your own.
Pick up your implement
and move on down that row.
Go on and sing while you're at it.
Might as well.

A WOMAN TELLS THE HISTORY OF HER PEOPLE

My body splits wide. Between the halves
lies the ocean my two great-great-grandfathers crossed
one way or another. This one from a western shore
of Africa, a pinpoint I will never find
along a thousand miles of maybe. That one
from a tiny town in Ireland which can be named
but will not be. In the loins of each
my ancestors formed, creatures rising from the sea
who walked upright days and years
to a small town in Alabama.
This is not a tender romance,
but a tale of swung axes and hunger.
A violence of water that baptized and tore
like one body that sheds its own skin
and enters by force the skin of another
the second remade in a stranger's image.

AMERICAN
HAPPINESS

THE VIOLENCE OF ORDINARY DAYS

The state of Alabama will electrocute Henry Francis Hays for beating a black man [Michael Donald] to death 16 years ago, and then hanging his body from a tree. . . It is a story of contrasts: The murderer, a white man, grew up in a home filled with hate and violence. The victim was reared by a loving mother and doting older siblings.
— FRANCES COLEMAN, *Mobile Register*, JUNE 1, 1997

When a rabbit, or anything else, bumping along the dark road dies under a wheel, the thrill is like taking a sharp turn into oncoming traffic, then off a bridge. Suddenly, I am the rabbit, scampering across the field; the hind leg of a bull bashes in my head. As I go down I see a boy, younger than Emmet Till, biking down the street. A gun falls from his pocket, discharges loudly. He picks it up, reloads, continues on his way. My car continues in a quick, ungraceful arc off the bridge, the Edmund Pettus Bridge, where marchers felt a rage of clubs and fists, a few dogs for good measure. Years later a woman stood on that historic bloody spot calling to a daughter a thousand miles away. Below her, the river is filled with bodies, their lips as blue as blue jays. She slipped across the rails as simply as the boy slipped more bullets in his gun, and my hand once slipped across my sister's open face for saying, "Bitch." I struck her twice, the feel of my palm against her skin, delicious, a silken purple scarf I feathered across your trusting neck. I might have killed you then, kicked you to a bloody pulp, hanged your body by the Krispy Kreme; instead, I left you for a banker, the same day Alabama put a wayward boy to death. Sorry, but this is who I am: a thoughtless woman who never swerves in time to save a rabbit, but drives on along the darkening road, the wounded in her wake.

THE KLAN PANHANDLES FOR DONATIONS AT THE INTERSECTION OF COURT STREET AND THE SOUTHERN BYPASS

Above the Southern Bypass, the Ku Klux Klan rose, a chimera
of white as white as my mother's sheets, swaying, even then, on
the other side of town. They held buckets out to cars, blessed
those who gave. And what blessings would they have for me
when I rolled up to the light? The old one looked right through
me. The young one thrust the bucket at my window, laughed,
and shook the coins. No absolution there. Lips curved, hoods
pointed to heaven, they were different from the wooden men I
imagined as a child. They were the cross, ablaze, on our front
lawn. Their *in hoc signo* for my mother's speech in a Selma
church. My mother put a sliver of the cross beneath her pillow;
my father put a loaded shotgun arms-reach from their bed. And
the K's, alliterating, strung them through my dreams from the
news to the lips of my Uncle Jeff *to get me*. Each night, square
jaws ground my name to sawdust until I could not sleep. Wooden
fingers tapped at my window, *to get me*. They were fire without
light, an unrelenting darkness, hidden in white laundry. And on
those summer evenings, when we sat gazing across our own back
yard, when neighbors shot their guns to say hello, my father did
not know I saw them in the trees. How could he have known?
How could I, a child in Tuskegee, Alabama, the shotguns calling
in the July darkness, have known that they were only this?—these
wooden men, tinder for my fire.

AMERICAN HAPPINESS

It used to be in Mayberry
folks were never colored
—not even black and white—
but beige, khaki,
a little gray. In Mayberry
Deputy Barney had one bullet
and no need for rope.
The only burning he did was for his Thelma Lou.
The sheriff had no gun,
just an Aunt Bea baking pies
and an Opie full of freckles heading off to fish
or sing or court. Whatever Opies do.
In Mayberry, no doors were barred or locked.
The jail was mostly empty.
The only water hose we ever saw
lay peacefully
curled
on Sheriff Andy's lawn.

Mayberry was a Southern town.
Technicolor must have killed it.
Made Andy a cranky lawyer.
Sent Opie running all the way to Hollywood.

But we remember.
Black and white,
from Chicago to Watts to Selma,
we tuned in to connect the dots of Opie's face
while we dined on mashed potatoes and buttered corn
right before our TV sets,
mesmerized,
that in this Southern town,
the sheriff used his hose to water Aunt Bea's roses.
We were so happy and relieved
we laughed until we could not think
until we fell off our sofas and wing-backs and cane-bottoms;
we laughed until we could not see or hear
until we could forget
that outside our own windows
other sheriffs with loaded guns, snarling dogs, and ready hoses
made quick work of a world on fire.

HOW TO SURVIVE AS A BLACK WOMAN
EVERYWHERE IN AMERICA
INCLUDING THE DEEP SOUTH

When a teacher, surefooted in her dominion,
ignores your raised arm, a single brown cane stalk
in the *ager* of Latin class, when she heaps praise
on Caesar and the little blonde *puella* who does not know
amo from *amas,* while alone in that cane field
you translate as if your life depends on
these dead words, do not protest when fear
and hatred show in eyes that look right through you,
do not pick up a fieldstone to knock
teacher's buck-toothed grin down her lily throat.
Say nothing, say nothing, say nothing.
Smile and put your hand down.
Smile and praise the little dumb girl.
Smile through every declination of your personhood.
Smiling is a lesson you can use.

When the man, so certain in his privilege,
turns to you in some reception line, inspects you
as if you stand on an auction block
and not the plush floor of the Renaissance Hotel,
when he laughs and says, "I heard
you were a Negro graduate student,"
except in genteel and colorless words,
when he questions you again and again,

hoping for affirmative action to show
its face, do not yell in righteous indignation of your smarts,
do not ask him some questions of your own, do not
shank him with your butter knife.
Say nothing, say nothing, say nothing.
Smile and answer his questions nonchalantly.
Smile when he says, "You are smart for a black girl."
Smile when he asks you to perform your monkey tricks,
for his wife, his friend, a passerby.
Monkey tricks might come in handy one day.

When your brown child goes walking down the street,
the hood of his ordinary sweatshirt pulled
low about his head, his pockets bulging with Skittles
and tea bottles, do not pretend you are surprised
when a man he has never seen accosts him
for thinking sidewalks are free for all.
When they bring his limp, brown body to your door,
and tell you how he brought it on himself,
was much, much too uppity to live, when they
praise the one who stood his ground and shot him dead,
do not scream and cry and cuss, do not
pick up your weapon and kill his killer, do not
blame the jurors for being blind.
Say nothing, say nothing, say nothing.
Smile and bury your only son.
Smile and calm the crazy crowd.
Smile and forgive, forgive, forgive.
Forgiveness covers centuries of sin.

When they knock, at last, at your own front door,
get up sure-footed from the bed you have made.
Get your children and your husband up too. Do not
stomp your feet in protest. Do not wave the cane stalk
of your arm in protest. Do not explain that you are
worthy and smart. Do not say you have sacrificed
enough. Go quietly into the trucks. Go quietly
into the long train cars. Go quietly
into the dark ovens, like the coward you are.

WHAT IF BARBIE WERE A REALITY TV STAR?

Barbie woke up irrelevant.
She could not go out
like that. She was over one billion sold,
beloved and such, not like Ken,
a has-been straight out the box.
Down at the corporate toy house she built,
she laid it out for a young exec so green
he had never even heard of Midge.
Six months later, Barbie reemerged
a new woman—Beyoncé-brown,
boobs so big her box had to be enlarged.
Little Asian children worked time and a half
to stitch in all that hair stolen from
unsuspecting Indian girls at the movies.
It was worth it.
Now, Barbie is queen again.
Made a basketball wife out of her.
Got her own reality show.
And *trending*—you better know.

ANOTHER THING TO WORRY ABOUT

Coyotes have moved into the garden district.
It's a good neighborhood, with mansions,
yards as old and leisurely as the money
that saves no one from bad luck or lightning

which kills thirty-seven people a year.
One-point-two million are maimed.
Seven people a day go up in flames.
It's a wonder the whole country is not filled

with walking wounded and graveyards.
We have learned Ebola cannot be contained
in remote regions any more than coyotes
who lounge in communal green spaces, prowling

for curious small dogs or
babies not unlike my own
who sat in the backseat or the one
nestled in my large belly when the cop

pulled me over that time. His body was rigid
with fury. Maybe coyotes had rattled
him. Everybody fears encroachment.
He hated mine into his road space. His hand

on his holstered gun made that clear.
How I wish I had bared my fangs
or made a low growl. I should have sprung
for his throat just like he sprang

up the hill much faster than the residential limit
and cut me off. My fault, he screamed,
as if offended by my presence on my own
street. Should I have forced my coyote

tongue to say, *You need to be more careful.*
Thirty-seven thousand die in car crashes
every year or entice him to bludgeon me
with *Black women are disproportionately*

jailed and sometimes beaten or worse with
no recourse? Anything but sit there silent
and still and afraid. He left me with a tongue-lashing
and another tick on my list. So many things

to worry about. One in three black men
will go to jail. I have two sons and one
husband. Which one will the odds come for?
One in two women will be sexually assaulted.

I have a daughter, a mother, and two sisters.
Even a coyote could do that math. I have stopped
watching the news. And now I read a woman
was attacked by a rabid raccoon as she was getting

in her car. Took her sons ten minutes to dislodge it
from her leg and beat it to death. It took days,
almost too many, to get the shot for its infectious
bite, the medicine being expensive and hard to come by.

THE STREET COMMITTEE MEETING
IS NOW IN SESSION

And then I said, "Whaattt?"
And she said, "Yeah, girl. That's what."
And I said, "For real, though?"
And she said, "Um, huh. For real."
And I said, "That's a shame."
And she said, "They don't know what shame is."
And I said, "What happened next?"
And she said, "You know what happened."
And I said, "Girl, no. Don't tell me that."
And she said, "Um, huh. You know how they are."
And I said, "Yeah, but you assume folks'll have some sense."
And she said, "Hmmph. You know what assuming gets you."
And I said, "Well, what did they say?"
And she said, "What could they say? Then they tried to get loud."
And I said, "Well, 'a hit dog'll holler.'"
And she said, "You know that's right."
And I said, "What is this world coming to?"
And she said, "Some kind of end I guess."
And I said, "You can say that again."
And she said, "Some kind of end."

ETHNOPHAULISM FOR THE NEWS

BALTIMORE CITY COUNCILMAN CARL STOKES'S
ANGRY RESPONSE TO CNN INTERVIEWER ERIN
BURNETT'S INSISTENCE ON REFERRING TO BLACK
RIOTERS AS THUGS:
"Just call them Niggers. Just call them Niggers."
— CNN, APRIL 28, 2015

Coons ran amok and burned down a CVS in Baltimore.

A gun collector opened fire on an SUV killing a young Spade for
    playing his music too loud. "I felt threatened," he said when
    asked why he had fired on the truckful of college Spades.

Statistics show a sharp increase in Porch Monkey-on-Porch
    Monkey crime. The National Science Foundation is funding
    studies of Porch Monkey brain pathology.

Policemen in Ferguson shot an unarmed Buck in the street. Other
    Bucks nationwide were outraged. Investigators found a long
    history of violence against Bucks, but officials noted the
    difficulty of keeping down the Buck population.

"This market has long been ignored," the CEO said as the
    world's largest cosmetics company launched its new line for
    natural Jungle Bunny hair. Products will appear in Ching
    Chong stores late August.

A twelve-year-old Pickaninny was killed by law enforcement when his toy gun was mistaken as real. On social media, citizens defended the police. "Pickanninies are dangerous." "You can't blame the cops for trying to defend themselves." What do you think? Tweet us @WVNS #pickaninny.

Stopped for a traffic violation, a Shine ran because he was late on his child support payments. The officer shot him in the back, killing him. "I felt threatened," the officer said of the fleeing Shine.

A Jigaboo has made history, winning the coveted award for best actress. "I am so honored to represent all the Jigaboos who never had this opportunity," she said. Her performance as Jezebel Jemima Brown chilled voters. "So authentic," said one Academy member.

Tarbaby and Spearchucker, joined by several local Darky leaders, met with President Touch-of-the-Tarbrush to discuss general unrest among the Spooks as of late. Leaders are encouraging local ordinances against sagging pants and proposing new education programs to civilize the Spooks. Tarbaby and Spearchucker will oversee distribution of funds.

In foreign news, Congress voted to increase military presence in the Middle East. "We've got to hit them now with everything we've got," said the Speaker of the House. "The Sand Nigga threat is real and growing."

GUN COLLECTOR SHOOTS UNARMED BLACK COLLEGE STUDENT FOR PLAYING MUSIC TOO LOUD

FLORIDA MAN PLEADS NOT GUILTY TO SHOOTING
TEEN TO DEATH OVER LOUD MUSIC

*"'It was loud,' Jacksonville homicide Lt. Rob
Schoonover said of the teens' music. 'They admit-
ted that. That's not a reason for someone to open
fire.'. . . 'His side of the story is he felt threatened
and that is the reason he took action,' Schoonover
said."*
— NBC NEWS ONLINE NOVEMBER 28, 2012

What was the man thinking
on the walk to the car
when he picked up the gun
raised, aimed, fired, the boy
slumped in the back seat? Did the evening news
play in his head? Did he see the housing project
he passes on his way to work, black boys draped
like cotton sacks on bannisters or leaning
in doorways smoking blunts? Was it the music
loud, indecipherable, urgent that manufactured
the absent gun, put it in the boy's hand, persuaded
the man to use his gun as one blind would use a stick

to find danger? What did the man think when the boy
took the bullets as freely as they were given? Did he see
the open hand, dead and brown, and empty? Did he see
the mother later looking at the hand?
Oh, my beloved country, what is to become of us,
caught as we are in our own imagined terror?

NO CHILD LEFT BEHIND

SPRING VALLEY HIGH SCHOOL OFFICER
SUSPENDED AFTER VIOLENT CLASSROOM ARREST
*"The student—who was released to her parents
after the incident—faces a charge of disturbing
schools, according to Wilson. Another female
student, Niya Kenny, faces the same charge after
allegedly standing up for the other teenager, her
mother, Doris Ballard, told CNN."*

— CNN.com

When she popped him, his mind blanked,
the mind version of brain freeze except
he forgot to stick his tongue
to roof of his mouth.
So he threw her
out of her desk, across the classroom
where learning must have taken place
at least that day. For those
who did not pay attention,
they could catch the rerun
on YouTube. How fast must a body fly
to make the teacher step back
to dodge the stain of blood or bone
on his black skin and white shirt?
Some say
she should have been less

transgressive like her great-grandmother
who would have known
to step off the sidewalk
or stand jubilant and silent
on command. That cop's foot in her back
was a teachable moment. Now she knows
she must close her mouth and lower her gaze
to divide or multiply justice.

BRIDGE CROSSING, SELMA, 2015

Strong men keep comin'
Strong men getting stronger

— STERLING BROWN

You stood on a bridge
named for a man who loved you
beneath his whip and foot. Rose up
a Grand Dragon to keep you there
just like the hooves of horses rose
that day to beat you down. Just like the clubs of men
rose to drive you back. Just like the tear gas,
those smoky ribbons, rose to make you weep.
And you walked and walked and walked
through blood and red clay, bramble
and years of ballots to listen to a man
who looked like you at a podium
of dragon bones. Did you imagine
you would return to this place
that hawks your pain and tears
for T-shirts and hotdogs?

EMMANUEL MEANS GOD IS WITH US

God was already there when the boy walked in.
When he heard the church door creak like his father's knees.
Still there when we prayed with him and he sat looking
into our eyes, brown pools of welcome like a summer
watering hole the boy knew once. The lift and heft
of the first gun his father gave him was so much to bear,
the Holy Spirit in his hands. God was standing there
when he almost changed his mind, then clean and quick
shot the pastor. Turned on his heel to the old women,
closed his heart and mind as one would close the Bible
after meditation. And God was there
when he learned to count. *Six little nigger boys*
playing with a hive; A bumblebee stung one
then there were five bodies halfway
to heaven. There, when he checked the bathroom,
the closets, under the pews. There still with *one little*
nigger boy left all alone.
Praise God, Christian nation, he was not
a racist. He did all he knew to do.
And God was watching.

Index of Poem Titles

Acknowledgments

With Gratitude and Love

THOUGH WRITING IS A solitary act, it most always occurs within a community. I certainly would never have been able to write this collection without being taken in and encouraged by family, friends, and strangers who cajoled, chastised, taught, and, most of all, cared enough about me and my poetry to listen. To my children, Jasmine, Joseph David II, and Joshua, you inspire me every day with your love, wisdom, and humor. Thank you for being mine. To Toi Derricote, Cornelius Eady, the fabulously talented Group B, the righteous faculty, and the rest of my Cave Canem family, there are not enough words for what you did for me. Thank you for your commitment to nurturing poetry, for allowing me in, and for providing me with a home where I may commune with the ancestors. To the Key West Writers Workshop program, thank you for the space to write and the amazing artist/teachers you provided to guide me. To my extraordinary teachers—Kenneth Deal, the first to tell me I could be a writer, rest in peace dear friend; Garrett Hongo, who taught me to take myself and my poetry seriously; Chase Twichell, who showed me the power of being meticulous; Marge Piercy, whose brilliance and insistence on knowing made me look at the world in new and expansive ways; Jane Hirschfield, who freed me to write a poem in thirty minutes, and Jericho Brown, whose masterful understanding of craft and strategy forever changed the way I read—thank you for making me a poet. To my Salon friends, you amazing artists—Foster, Joey, Eileen, Caroline, Tom, Catherine, Janet, Jim, David, Mark, Camilla, and Joseph—your faithfulness, kindness, and support have been an oasis in the desert. To my writing family—Honoree Jeffers, Jeanie Thompson, Jennifer Fremlin, Neal Lester, Trudier Harris, and Jennifer Horne—thank you for reading my work and for your steadfast encouragement. To Randall Williams and Suzanne La Rosa, thank you for your sincere faith in me and your patience. To the many, many others whose generosity and unwavering support provided me with the physical, psychical, and emotional space to complete this manuscript, I thank you. And finally, "Thanks be to God for His indescribable gift!" (2 Corinthians 9:15 NAS). Peace.

About the Author

JACQUELINE ALLEN TRIMBLE lives and writes in Montgomery, Alabama, where she is an associate professor of English and chairperson of Languages and Literatures at Alabama State University. Her work has appeared in various online and print publications including *The Griot*, *The Offing*, and *The Blue Lake Review*. She is currently a Cave Canem fellow and the recipient of a 2017 literary arts fellowship from the Alabama State Council on the Arts.